CERRILLOS

YESTERDAY, TODAY AND TOMORROW

The Story of a Won't-Be Ghost Town

by

Jacqueline E. Lawson

Sunstone Press
Santa Fe, New Mexico

First Edition

Printed in the United States of America

Library of Congress Cataloging in Publication Data:

Lawson, Jacqueline E., 1928-
    Cerrillos : yesterday, today, and tomorrow : the story of a won't be
ghost town / by Jacqueline E. Lawson. -- /st ed.
      p.   cm.
    Bibliography: p.
    Includes index.
    ISBN: 0-86534-130-3 : $ 8.95
    1. Los Cerrillos (N.M.) -- History.   I. Title.
F804.L62L38   1989
978-9'56--dc19   88-34578

Published in 1989 by SUNSTONE PRESS
Post Office Box 2321
Santa Fe, NM 87504-2321 / USA

TABLE OF CONTENTS

PREFACE

It was only a few years ago that I visited Cerrillos, New Mexico, for the first time. But I can still recall my first morning there when I was awakened by the penetrating stillness of unfamiliar surroundings.

My stroll outside that first day was limited to a few yards from the house where I was staying. The next day, however, I decided to brave more of the village. I had arrived in Cerrillos at dusk and therefore was unsure as to what I would encounter during my visit. Attempting to appear casual walking up the road from the house, I tried to ignore the dogs that barked or sauntered up to sniff at the squeak of my new western boots. The camera slung over my shoulder was sure to mark me as a tourist, but I wanted to be prepared for the unusual in my first ghost town visit.

As I walked carefully along the rock-encrusted streets — there were no sidewalks — a couple of small children peered from behind the protective shelter of a broken fence gate and a tractor part. I felt inquiring eyes peeking from the windows behind fragmented curtains as I made my way up the road: Past rusted automobiles, crumbling adobe walls, partially-hidden frame and adobe structures, wildly-growing brush in what appeared to be front yards, and rough-hewed picket fences, all of which reinforced my feeling that the residents probably wanted to be left alone.

Then I finally came to the main street where I was met with an imposing sight — a church whose magnificence seemed to dare one to scoff at its village.

Looking up the street past the church was the scene I had missed the evening of my arrival. Had it not been for a couple of parked cars, I would have thought I was back in the days of the 1800s when "men were men." I almost expected to see a herd of cattle coming down the dusty road ahead, or perhaps a cowboy sitting lazily in the saddle urging his horse to move on.

Passing by the church I went on down the street and must admit relief at the sight of Mary and Leo in their corner bar. There I soon became engaged in a few words of chitchat with a young prospector who invited me to play a game of pool. I had never played pool before, and proved it. Declining an invitation for a second game, I left the bar and went next door to Mitch's What-Not Shop. The vastness of the variety and amount of Mitch's wares was too overwhelming to take in this first day. So after a brief conversation with the owner, I purchased a turquoise ring and left. I retraced my steps past the bar, crossed the street, and saw the "Open" sign in front of what appeared to be a general store which had apparently been closed when I passed it earlier. I went in to buy a pack of cigarettes and was cheerfully greeted by the Simoni sisters who invited me to sit awhile and have a can of beer.

Main Street, from Church

As I was alone and had no car, it was obvious I was staying somewhere in Cerrillos. But no one asked me who I was visiting, or why I was in Cerrillos. They merely made the usual resident-to-visitor small talk with me, and I was soon put at ease. But from almost everyone I spoke with, there was some mention of the past: "You should have seen . . ."; "Once there was . . "; "There used to be . . " I got bits and pieces about the Palace Hotel, Tiffanys, the Opera House, the old school. It was just enough to make me realize that there had been more to Cerrillos than met the eye. I suddenly had the desire to know what used to be behind the crumbling adobe ruins.

I soon found that the libraries had numerous historical articles describing the Los Cerrillos mining district and the original Indian inhabitants. In the few describing the village of Cerrillos, almost each one emphasized its twenty-six saloons and three or four hotels. Rumored exploits of local infamous folks like Black Jack Ketchum, Choctaw Kelly, and Broncho Mary were highlighted in nearly every article I read (although I was never able to substantiate their direct connections with Cerrillos). Some did mention homesteaders of the village of Cerrillos such as the Richard Greens, D.D. Harkness, William Hurt. But suddenly it was as if Cerrillos ceased to exist.

There were a few later articles in local magazines and newspapers by former residents reminiscing their past. Even these dealt with Cerrillos as if it no longer existed — a place that had already given up the ghost and was merely a dusty once-was and no-longer-is town. At my first visit, I felt somewhat the same way. But after two or three successive visits within a few months of each other, I began to wonder just how dead was this town. Talking with Mary and Leo at the bar, with Mitch at his What-Not Shop, with the Simoni sisters, and with Fran, the last owner of the Tiffany Saloon, I was impressed by their expressions of hopes of Cerrillos coming back to life and their ideas on how this could come about. So my interest in the past of Cerrillos developed into a search for its future.

My research began in the New Mexico State Archives in Santa Fe. I discovered that there had been booming business houses (in addition to the oft-mentioned saloons); buildings and owners that changed trades from year to year as the need arose; families that prospered and some that died out or just disappeared.

As my return visits to Cerrillos increased, the townsfolk became more used to my camera and my obvious interest in and concern about their town. At first my interviews were limited to casual conversation, lest I frighten them off. Before too long, however, I was being treated like a member of a Cerrillos family. Each time I returned, I was welcomed like a long-lost relative by the three or four households I became close to. Much of my story is theirs.

ACKNOWLEDGEMENTS

Anyone can look through history books and old newspaper articles and come up with a few facts, but without the personal input of living persons, facts are nothing more than dull words when put down on paper.

In this light, I wish to express my gratitude to the following individuals for their time, interest and sharing of tidbits and photographs without which this publication could not have taken place: Fran Eckols, Emma Simoni Montoya, Mary (Tappero) and Leo Mora, Joe Sahd, Corinna Simoni, Edith Simoni, Patra Smith, and Julia Vergolio Weeks. They were the suppliers of the "meat" of my story. Through them, I was able to walk down Cerrillos streets of the early 1900s, peer through the windows of buildings long gone, and gossip with school children of the past.

However, without the facts, there would be no story to write. For these, I will be ever grateful to Orlando Romero of the New Mexico Historical Library, Al Regenberg of the New Mexico State Archives, and Britt Kaur of the Denver Public Library for their patience, insight, and knowledge of resources.

And for the thoughtful review of my manuscript before publication, my thanks go to Fran Eckols whose Tiffany Saloon will never be forgotten by the townsfolk.

The one person, however, whose enthusiasm and support inspired me from the beginning was my host on that first visit, David G. Kaufman. His sensitivity for and perception about people taught me to learn to look beyond today to "smell the roses" of the past and the future. Without his encouragement, this project would never have been completed. Thanks, David.

INTRODUCTION

Cerrillos, New Mexico, is located approximately twenty-five miles southwest of downtown Santa Fe, just off New Mexico Highway 14, and sits at an elevation of 5,688 feet. Some maps and literature still identify this community by its original name, Los Cerrillos, the little hills.

The main section of Cerrillos is located between the San Marcos and the Galisteo Arroyos, with the railroad tracks dividing off about one-fifth of the village.

There is another section of residences south of the Galisteo Arroyo. As a reminder of the past, the skeletal remains of the once-grand school structure, built in 1892, still stands in this section.

For many years, Cerrillos was almost like an island, as it was surrounded on three sides by arroyos which were the only roads in and out. Before the Galisteo River changed course, there were times of the year when the arroyos were filled by flash floods, allowing an exit possible only north over the mine-encrusted hills.

In most publications mentioning Cerrillos since the 1940s, it is described as one of the ghost towns of New Mexico. One dictionary defines a ghost town as a town permanently abandoned by its inhabitants. Cerrillos is not permanently abandoned as there are over one hundred land owners who continue to call that little village home.

The last of the more productive mines has recently closed, but there still remain those families and individuals who will not give up their serenity and seclusion for the way of the big city.

This is the story of one so-called ghost town, but it mirrors that of thousands of similar settlements all across the country: boom towns that started with the discovery of precious metals, then grew with the expanding railroad system. And as the gold and silver petered out and the prospectors and miners moved on, the businessmen left, taking their wares elsewhere. Families were forced to abandon their homes and the town — more or less to nature's way — leaving only a few hardy souls who kept hoping things would pick up again some day.

The state of New Mexico is dotted with a countless number of these places. Its history of the riches disclosed over three hundred years ago and still being sought is unique among the States. What still lies undiscovered in the little rolling hills, behind and beneath pueblo ruins may never be revealed.

In the pages that follow, you are invited to stroll down the dirt streets of Cerrillos, return to the old days as they probably were, then come back to the present and enjoy the now days as they are or soon hope to be.

I. THE BEGINNINGS

More than two thousand years ago, Indians found deposits of pale blue rock, described as chalchihuitl, in the little hills (los cerrillos) located in the north central part of the state of New Mexico. This rock, now called turquoise, was highly valued by the Indians as a sacred stone capable of protecting its bearer from evil. Turquoise was said to have been used to brace the walls of the pueblos and can still occasionally be found imbedded in the outside walls of adobe structures.

Invading Spaniards soon discovered other valuable ores, silver and gold, and used the Indians as slave labor to excavate these metals, as well as the turquoise, for exportation to Spain. One of the primary sites of excavation of the precious stones was from the Mina del Tiro (Mine of the Shaft), located at Mt. Chalchihuitl. It was during one of the major excavations that the entire west face of the mountain caved in burying many of the Indian laborers. It is believed that this incident was one of the principal causes of the Indians' rebellion against the Spanish in 1680.

Over the next two centuries, these deposits lay more or less dormant, although some determined prospectors were able to come up with occasional small strikes. The Spanish did return to the area in the late 1690s to seek the mines containing lead which they needed for bullets. Subsequently, they staked claims for silver, and in the late 1700s grants were registered for land containing turquoise.

Prospecting in the early 1800s unearthed the gold, with one of the larger lodes located on the Jose Francisco Ortiz land grant. Until 1866, the region had been closed to citizens of the United States. Once it was opened to the Americans, the riches began to reveal themselves once again to persistent prospectors.

Public Land Sale

In May 1879 President U.S. Grant offered a public sale of lands in New Mexico that included the boundaries of Los Cerrillos. Stephen Elkins, an enterprising political figure, took advantage of first-hand knowledge of the valuable past and speculative future of these lands. Together with a partner he began to accumulate property by settling land disputes, and then making whatever arrangements were necessary to secure the land.

The Boom

Later in 1879 the discovery by miners from Leadville, Colorado, of the old Indian lodes containing zinc, lead and silver in those little hills near Mt. Chalchihuitl started a boom that enticed would-be miners and prospectors from all over the country. In addition, tent towns of gold seekers sprang up all along the beds of the streams that flowed through the arroyos of this area — now the Los Cerrillos and Galisteo Mining Districts. As one writer described the scene, the channels of the larger streams appeared to be "one vast sluice box," with prospectors sifting out the gold which had collected between the rocks on the river beds.

In the surrounding hills excavations appeared everywhere as new claims were staked. It was not long before the districts were peppered with mine shafts developed from 10 to 340 feet deep. The old Mina del Tiro exuded the once lost silver ore; Mt. Chalchihuitl released its turquoise at the old Spanish Turquoise Mine. Large strikes at the Cash Entry produced silver as well as gold and copper. The old Ortiz Mine was the site of one of the more prominent open pit-leaching operations. Other digs revealed zinc, lead, and iron.

Hundreds of mining claims appeared, although many undoubtedly produced nothing more than financial losses and subsequent tragedy for their owners.

Atchison, Topeka & Santa Fe Railroad

Richard L. Wootton owned the toll road over the only suitable route through the mountains over Raton Pass for the railroad to continue from Colorado into New Mexico. Right-of-way had been obtained by the chief engineer in February 1877 for the Atchison, Topeka and Santa Fe (AT&SF) railroad. The first railroad town in New Mexico was Otero, founded by the AT&SF in March 1879. The line from Santa Fe to Lamy was established in Feburary 1880. Then on April 15, 1880 the line to Albuquerque, which went through the Los Cerrillos camp, was opened.

The AT&SF soon set up Los Cerrillos Station as the supply center for the surrounding mining camps — Waldo, Madrid, Golden, San Pedro, and Dolores. Construction of the station building at Los Cerrillos began in February 1881.

Although the mining of silver, gold and turquoise had played an extensive role in the building of the Los Cerrillos mining district, it was the coal found near Waldo, and later Madrid, New Mexico, that was the principal mineral product to bring prosperity to the soon-to-be town of Cerrillos.

Major bituminous coal workings were developed near Waldo. For this reason, beehive ovens used to convert coal products to coke were constructed at Waldo which was three miles south of Cerrillos on the railroad line. The mines in Madrid had been worked as early as 1869 by the New Mexico Mining Company. Testing eventually revealed that the coal found in the Madrid area was the best outside of the state of Pennsylvania. The distance of Madrid from a railroad shipping point, however, restricted its coal market to towns in the immediate area where coal could be distributed by wagon. As coal was the supplier of fuel for the railroad steam engines, acquisition of ownership of these mines was a major goal of the AT&SF Railroad. In 1891 the AT&SF took possession of the coal mining property at Madrid and installed a spur line from there to Waldo.

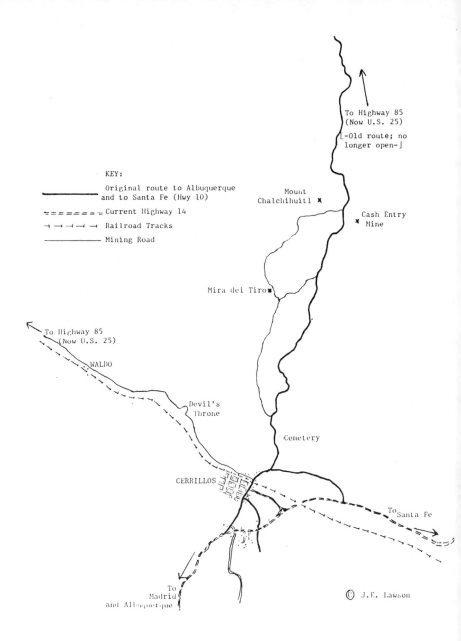

KEY:

——————— Original route to Albuquerque and to Santa Fe (Hwy 10)

= = = = = = = Current Highway 14

⊣ ⟶ ⊣ ⟶ ⊣ ⟶ ⟶ Railroad Tracks

——————— Mining Road

To Highway 85 (Now U.S. 25)

[-Old route; no longer open-]

Mount Chalchihuitl ✗

Cash Entry ✗ Mine

Mira del Tiro ✗

To Highway 85 (Now U.S. 25)

WALDO

Devil's Throne

Cemetery

CERRILLOS

To Santa Fe

To Madrid and Albuquerque

© J.E. Lawson

13

II. EVOLUTION OF A TOWN

With little difficulty, the eager new land owner, Mr. Elkins, was able to sell off his now-valuable property to business men and women who began to appear in Los Cerrillos Station, now known as the village of Cerrillos, some bringing with them their entire families. Tent dwellings were soon replaced by houses.

> One particularly aspiring developer, D.D. Harkness, purchased lots adjacent to the railroad tracks in 1880 with the intention of building a hotel. He then erected a temporary building as a home for his family while he worked in the mines. One day, according to the story, he came home to find that his wife had opened up their home to provide room and board for the AT&SF workers who were laying railroad tracks in the area. This first "bed-and-breakfast" establishment soon built up to become an eighteen-room hotel which the Harknesses called the Cerrillos House, a competitor with C.W. Uptegrove's Tabor House (later the Grand Central Hotel), the first formal hotel in Cerrillos.

Cerrillos had its first post office in January 1880, with the postmaster being George A. Waller. The post office itself changed location with each change of postmasters, eight from January 1881 through February 1900.

As with other mining boom towns, Cerrillos continued to grow steadily over the next few years. Men from Santa Fe set up branches of their businesses in the new town of Cerrillos: Abe Spiegelberg's Meat Market. J.H. Gerdes's Clothing Store, Z. Staab's General Merchandise, W.A. McKenzie's Hardware, Weltmer's Stationery and Book Store.

The most prominent and numerous buinesses were saloons. By the number of saloons that existed at the same time, said to have been as many as twenty-six, business must have been good. With the rich deposits of coal being mined in the immediate proximity, Cerrillos was now being referred to as the "little Pittsburg."

In January 1882 a town council was elected, and D.D. Harkness was chosen as justice of the peace. Population was about 300, increasing almost daily.

By 1883, landowners realized the time was ripe to sell off their property across the Galisteo River arroyo in the area called "Otro Lado" (other side) by local townspeople. Making plans for further development of Cerrillos, a group of businessmen calling themselves the Cerrillos Town Company plotted nearly 400 lots in the new area. In June 1884 the plans had progressed to such an extent that a map of the lots was drawn up by the George F. Nesbitt Company of New York. Streets were assigned names such as Albuquerque, Placer, and Ortiz Avenues. Circulars were prepared by the *Santa Fe New Mexico Review* for distribution all over the country, describing the advantages of living in the Cerrillos area.

Lot Sale

Why there was a delay in transactions is uncertain, but finally, by 1887, the Cerrillos Town Company was ready for the big sale of lots.

An auction was held on 7 July 1887 by Captain John Gray, William Berger and Judge L. Bradford Prince for the sale of 100 of the lots plotted across the arroyo. The auction continued after dark, and when it was terminated at about 9:30 p.m., they found that 105 lots had been sold — 5 more than were available — for a total of $3,086. Purchasers were primarily from Santa Fe and Cerrillos. Among the Cerrillos bidders were Tony Neis, W.C. Hurt, D.D. Harkness, Dr. Joseph Richards, and C.W. Uptegrove.

The Cerrillos Town Company donated lots in this section for three new churches. There was also a site included for a new school. Homes did appear on the south side of the Galisteo River arroyo, and in later years the school was built there. The major businesses and activities remained on the north side.

Although Cerrillos already had at least two hotels and a boarding house, the little boom town continued to need temporary housing for its ongoing influx of new residents. In 1888, what was to become a landmark in the town of Cerrillos for the next eighty years was constructed by newcomers to the area, Mr. and Mrs. Richard Green and their family of eleven children, The Palace Hotel.

The dirt roads in front of the businesses and homes remained dirt roads; and although few residents realized it, they did have official names.

Street Names

Railroad Avenue was, of course, the road that paralleled the railroad tracks. The next street was the first cross street reached when entering Cerrillos from the original highway. In the early days it held most of the businesses, so it was called *Main Street.*

The next parallel street was *Waldo Street,* probably named after the town of Waldo which was the next train stop south of Cerrillos.

The third street was given the name of *River Street* as it paralleled the Galisteo River. Some residents called it "La Chaparral" possibly because of the dense growth of trees and shrubs enveloping the road.

On the north side of Railroad Avenue, as far as is known only the first parallel street was named: It was *Richards,* possibly after Dr. Joseph Richards, pharmacist, landowner, and later postmaster.

The first north-south street in Cerrillos was identified as First Street, with the next two parallel streets appropriately named *Second* and *Third Streets.* Following Third was the Galisteo Arroyo which skirted the town on nearly three sides.

For a time, the road from Santa Fe to Madrid (the original Highway 10) passed right through Cerrillos on First Street. As the highway continued on to cross the bridge over the Galisteo River, First Street was sometimes called "Bridge Street." (See Highways and Bridges.)

"Metropolitan" Cerrillos continued to grow, by 1890 having had more than its share of saloons, its fourth postmaster, and all of the other amenities of the big city, including "houses of ill fame."

Fire

Then on June 23, 1890 fire destroyed a block (described as Block 9) of businesses located on South Railroad Avenue between First and Second Streets.

The *Santa Fe New Mexican Daily* reported that the village burned "from Hogan's to the Cerrillos house." It originated in a two-story frame building, known as the Spiegelberg Building, then owned by W.C. Hurt, located nearly across from the railroad station building.

The fire was contained within that block and did not cross Second to reach the *Rustler* office (assumed to have been on the corner) nor the Cerrillos House Hotel next to it. The newspaper concluded its report by stating that "it is very generally believed that the fire was of incendiary origin."

Of the estimated loss of $30,000, nearly $18,000 was covered by insurance. Within a few months, several of the businesses were rebuilt.

Cerrillos was incorporated in 1891, at which time it was said to have had a population of 1,000. Some writers had placed the 1890 population figure as high as 2,500.

Highways and Bridges

The original wagon road from the north to Cerrillos was the Mina del Tiro arroyo. The road entered town over the railroad tracks via First Street. It continued through Cerrillos to Waldo Street where it turned southeast to meet the Galisteo Arroyo. There it was connected to the other side by way of a bridge. The road then continued on over the hills to Madrid.

With the flash floods and the continuous change of pattern of the Galisteo River, the bridge was continuously being washed out and in a state of poor repair. By 1887 the citizens decided to have a real bridge constructed without the aid of the county. Finally, in 1893 enough road taxes had been collected so that the Town Council was able to award a contract for this new bridge to be erected at the end of First Street. Eventually, the citizens did have to seek help from the county. In September 1897 County Commissioners appropriated $100 and the Town Council matched this amount for the building of the new bridge.

In August 1898 the Town Council appropriated forty dollars "for the purpose of putting a floor on the foot-bridge across the Galisteo." Finally in May 1900 a contract was awarded to two local men to "take down the cable and lumber" from what was left of the old bridge.

In October 1901 John Cheapuso's bid to build the new bridge was accepted by the Town Council, and final bills for the construction were paid that December. Unfortunately, the new bridge also succumbed to the ever-changing course of the river, and the cement pillars sank into the sandy river bed almost overnight. The remaining pillars of this "white bridge" can still be seen from the south side of the arroyo. The Highway Department eventually constructed the new highway and bridge, bypassing the town of Cerrillos.

Bridge pillars

Schools

The first school in Cerrillos was located across the railroad tracks at Second and Richards in a house donated by D.D. Harkness, C.W. Uptegrove, and others in 1883. By 1891, however, whatever school facility Cerrillos had was becoming too small to accommodate the growing population of children.

In September 1892 a new two-story brick school was constructed on the south side of the arroyo. The first floor was the grade school; the second story was for high school students.

The first principal of this new school was John Barnhard, with Professor Flavio Silva as instructor for the Spanish-speaking children. In 1906 Dr. Friend Palmer, the town physician, was president of the school board, and Miss B.K. Gilday was the school teacher. A later principal was Mrs. McCrow, with Mrs. Kelly as school teacher. (Three of Cerrillos's current residents, E.J. Mitchell, Mary Mora, and Joe Sahd, taught in that school in the 1950s and 1960s.)

While the Galisteo River foot-bridge was still intact, the school children had a direct walking route to the school. After both bridges were washed out, however, they had to make their way to school walking on planks which their parents set up in the dry or muddy and often wet bed of the arroyo. The changing course of the river had caused the river bed to widen such that the flow of water was barely a trickle except during the time of the seasonal flash floods which usually occurred in August.

The 1890s appeared to be the prime years of Cerrillos, with its three or four hotels, still over twenty saloons, restaurants, meat markets and grocery stores, barber shops and bakeries, dance halls, and a theater. There was even a jail as early as September 1891, referred to in Town Council minutes as the "town prison." Three major newspapers had been published.

Newspapers
The first weekly newspaper, *The Los Cerrillos Prospector*, edited by A.V. Aoy in Carbonateville, was in Spanish and English, and continued publication from July 4, 1879 to 1881. It was moved to Cerrillos sometime during those three years.

The first publication of the next newspaper, *The Cerrillos Rustler*, was on July 27, 1888 by F.C. Buell.

On June 20, 1891 G.M. Hormer published the first edition of his weekly newspaper, *The Cerrillos Beacon*, in competition with *The Cerrillos Rustler*. The *Beacon* lasted only six months, whereas the *Rustler* continued publication in Cerrillos for about ten years.

There were also other short-lived publications: The *Chronicle*, the *Comet*, and the *Register*.

The *La Turquesa* was a newspaper published in later years by the high school principal, Mrs. McCrow.

Electricity
Electricity was first introduced to Cerrillos in 1901. Plans were made for power to be supplied by the Cochiti Gold Mining Company's electric plant at Madrid three miles south. According to the *Santa Fe New Mexican*, the wiring was to be done by "Messrs. Porter and Pruitt."

By 1902 the smelter (described later) did have electricity, but it was over forty years before Cerrillos homes were finally supplied electric lights.

In 1905 a telephone line was operating from Santa Fe to Cerrillos.

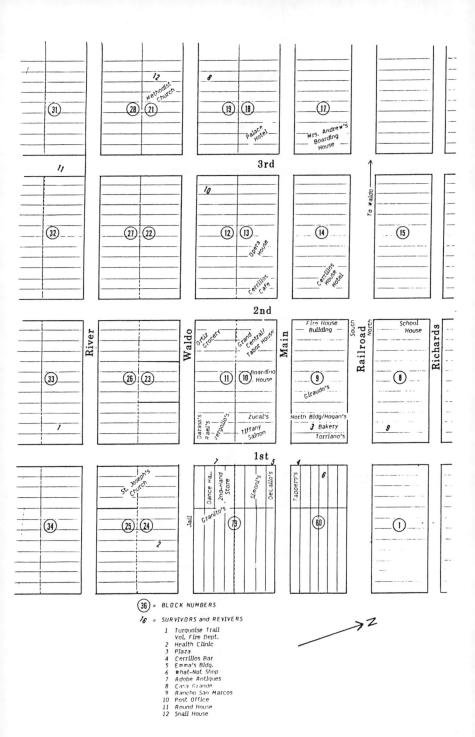

3rd

2nd

1st

River

Waldo

Main

Railroad

Richards

To Waldo

South   North

Methodist Church

Palace Hotel

Mrs. Andrew's Boarding House

Opera House

Cerrillos Cafe

Cerrillos House Hotel

Ortiz Grocery

Grand Central Tabor House

Fire House Building

School House

Boarding House

Giraudo's

Darasis's

Rael's

Vergollo's

Zucal's

Tiffany Saloon

North Bldg/Hogan's

3 Bakery

Torriano's

St. Joseph's Church

Jail

Dance Hall

Granito's

2nd-Hand Store

Simoni's

DeLallo's

Tapper's

① = BLOCK NUMBERS

16 = SURVIVORS and REVIVERS

1 Turquoise Trail Vol. Fire Dept.
2 Health Clinic
3 Plaza
4 Cerrillos Bar
5 Emma's Bldg.
6 What-Not Shop
7 Adobe Antiques
8 Casa Grande
9 Rancho San Marcos
10 Post Office
11 Round House
12 Snail House

→ Z

21

III. WALKING THROUGH OLD CERRILLOS

Main Street at First

Through the years, the booming ecomony of Cerrillos resulted in frequent changes of the business enterprises in the buildings. Major business establishments were contained in the first three lots on the south side of Main Street beginning at First.

Owned by Stephen B. Elkins, the first lot was sold to George and Ida North in 1889. Although it has been reported that the original building was erected some twenty years prior, in 1889 the Norths built an adobe structure the entire length and width of the property: 25 feet by 100 feet. On Lot 2 the owner built a house, and the building on Lot 3 was a store. During the years the Norths' corner building housed a furniture and hardware store, and eventually a saloon.

In 1907 James P. NcNulty purchased the first two lots, paying $2,570 for the first property and $1,950 for the second. Mr. McNulty was, at that time, the manager of the turquoise mines for the American Turquoise Company. He was also the mine manager for the Tiffany people of New York. It is likely that Mr. McNulty gave the name "Tiffany" to the eventual saloon on the corner.

Tiffany Saloon.

After Mr. McNulty's five-year ownership came Cipriano Lucero, followed by Joe Juliano. The next two owners, Joe Zucal and Jay Coyle, also ran the grocery store in the building on the third lot. A later owner converted the corner saloon into a restaurant.

Tiffany (Fran Eckols & Nadine Heiden)

From left to right: Brijado Montoya, Pete Garcia, Gene Montoya.

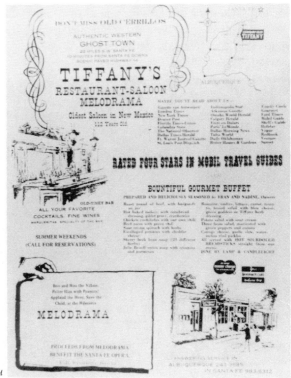

Tiffany menu

The owner in 1958, Warren Sands, sold the Tiffany property to two ambitious women, Fran Eckols and Nadine Heiden.

> *Miss Eckols had been co-owner of a similar place of business in Anchorage, Alaska. The two women's most recent venture was in advertising in Texas. Under their guidance, this new business was opened in about 1962 and flourished both as a local place of entertainment and as a tourist attraction, delighting many famous guests, including movie stars and opera personalities, most of whom remained Tiffany devotees during the years.*

Miss Eckols and Miss Heiden converted the grocery store into the Tiffany Melodrama Theater which attracted participating actors from Santa Fe and Albuquerque.

> *Beatrice Kay made at least two guest appearances at the Theater. The Tiffany Restaurant became the first four-star restaurant in New Mexico, and was even advertised as New Mexico's "oldest saloon." The special cuisine and nostalic interior depicted the Gay 90s.*

In later years they leased the building next to the Simoni Store (described later), calling it the Starlight Cabaret. Here groups from Santa Fe and elsewhere held musical presentations for the entertainment of the Tiffany Restaurant patrons.

The Tiffany Restaurant-Saloon-Melodrama Theater met its demise March 15, 1977 when the business portion of the property was consumed by fire. As the business had been an influential tourist attraction as well as an employer of Cerrillos residents, its loss had a major adverse impact on the economy of Cerrillos.

Tiffany Saloon inside

24

Tiffany Restaurant inside

West Side of First Street, Main towards Waldo Street

On First Street south of the Tiffany Saloon in about 1915 were Joe Vergolio's businesses: A grocery-general merchandise store and a bakery which he later converted into a saloon. The Vergolios had living quarters in back of the grocery store.

In the house next to Vergolio's bakery lived the Ciraco Rael family The corner building at Waldo Street was Louie Darass's bar and later Rael's meat market and shoe repair shop from about 1915 to 1923.

> *In about 1905, Mr. Vergolio planted three cottonwood trees on this corner: One on First Street, and two others around the corner on Waldo. (Two of these trees are still standing.) Mr. Darass "paid" Mr. Vergolio a glass of beer for each tree he planted.*

Vergolio trees, Winter

Vergolio trees, Spring

Down Main Street, from First

Back on Main Street and First, during Joe Zucal's ownership of the Tiffany, the third building from the corner on Main Street was his grocery and general merchandise store from 1922 to the 1940s.

> *It took some effort to keep grocery stores stocked in the early days of Cerrillos, and many of the families needing to make purchases had rather meager means. So it was not unusual for the Zucals to sell tomatoes by the slice. A later grocery even sold cloves by the "each," according to a recent resident.*

Still later owner Jay Coyle called his grocery store "Fancy Foods." The next building was eventually occupied by Sandoval's barber shop. Two doors down was a 2-story boarding house, then H.C. Yontz's Jewelry Store.

Yontz's Jewelry Store

Cerrillos's first major hotel was C.W. Uptegrove's Tabor House Hotel. Located down on the corner of Main and Second Streets, it was also used as a meeting place for the town council on occasion. The building was enlarged and renamed the Grand Central Hotel by Mr. Uptegrove in 1890. Owned by W.C. Rogers in 1893, it was later called the Roger Hotel (in 1898). By 1902 it was again being called the Central Hotel.

The corner building across Second Street was erected sometime between 1893 and 1897. In 1898 it was a meat market. It is assumed that through the

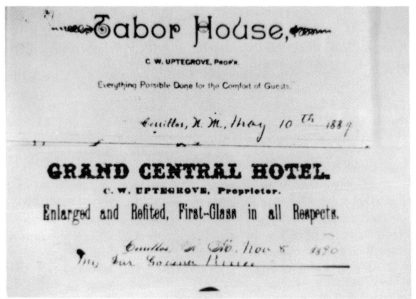

Uptegrove's letterheads

early years, this building remained a meat market or perhaps a general food store. Owner in 1915 was John Mutto. In later years that building and the adjoining property on Second Street was purchased by the Sahd family. Joe Sahd developed the corner building into a restaurant, and at one time it was called the Turquesa Cafe.

The business was leased from Mr. Sahd in 1974 by Grace (Card) Schmitt who operated it as the Card House Restaurant. Ms. Schmitt was a board member of the Concerned Citizens for Cerrillos, a quasi town council, and town meetings were held at her restaurant.

In 1978 the restaurant was leased by Deborah Pine and Julie L. Dunn who operated their new Cerrillos Cafe for a few years as a home-style restaurant.

The Opera House

Down from the Cerrillos Cafe, on Main Street, was the Opera House. Originally owned by Stephen Elkins, the property was sold in 1881 to A.W. Pollan and L.S. Butterfield. It was later purchased by William C. Hurt who bought adjoining lots in 1888 from J.R. Silva. The Hurt family had settled in Cerrillos in about 1881, and through the years they became extensive property owners in Cerrillos.

Also known as Hurt's Hall, the Opera House was used for community entertainment such as dances and theatrical presentations.

The 20 June 1891 Cerrillos Beacon described a performance at the Opera House of a comedy, "Early Years," by local actors. The 29 June 1894 Cerrillos Rustler told readers of the successful ball held the previous Friday at Hurt's Hall. It is believed that Sarah Bernhardt once performed there.

A few years after Mr. Hurt's death in 1889, his widow, Maud, deeded the building to the Masons (in 1903), where it served as one of the first Masonic lodges in the state of New Mexico. (The lodge was moved to Santa Fe in 1952 and is still known as the Cerrillos Masonic Lodge No. 19.)

The Opera House building was sold by the Masons to Mary Salazar in 1952. In 1974 it was a private residence whose owner operated a coffee house in the front for a brief time.

The building was placed on the New Mexico State Register of Cultural Properties in March 1974. It was after that time that the overhang and its pillars at the entrance decayed such that they had to be removed for safety. Then the bricks that lay at the base of the pillars gradually found their way into other local structures.

In 1977 the interior of the old Opera House was transformed as its new owner, Baird Banner, built within its walls a modern recording studio. To prevent vandalism to the interior, the owner removed the rotting entrance door and replaced it with stone closely matching the remainder of the outside of the building.

In the remainder of the block was the home of Tony and Catarina Tappero, purchased by them in 1917.

Palace Hotel

Mr. and Mrs. Richard Green and family, who had migrated from Texas with their herd of cattle, settled in San Pedro, New Mexico in 1884. With the nearest school being in Cerrillos, and eleven children in the Green family, however, they decided to move on to Cerrillos where, in 1885, they made their home in a seven-room structure which purportedly had been built in 1827 as a stagecoach stop and later used as a trading post.

At a cost to Mr. Green quoted as being $10,000, in 1888 he utilized Cochiti Indian labor to add five more rooms to this house. The Indians made each adobe brick for the addition by hand. This elegant structure on the corner of Main at Third Street soon became the Palace Hotel.

A detailed description, by Nancy Green McCleary, of the Green family and the Palace Hotel can be found in the "Foreword" to the publication, Cerrillos Adventure at the Bar T H Ranch, by Maggie Day Trigg. According to Mrs. McCleary, rumored notable guests did stay at the Palace Hotel: Thomas A. Edison, Ulysses S. Grant, then General, and New Mexico's Governor L. Bradford Prince. In addition, a daughter of the Vergolios, later Palace Hotel owners, saw the names of Sarah Bernhart and Lew Wallace listed in the hotel register.

Palace Hotel (side)

Palace Hotel (front)

One long-time resident of the Palace Hotel was Julius Muralter whose tailor shop was located on the first floor of the new adobe section. He remained in business there for over twenty-two years. Another long-time boarder was the town physician, Dr. Friend Palmer, whose office was above

Mr. Muralter's shop. The office of a dentist, Dr. William Bishop, was also on the second floor.

The Cerrillos Masons occupied a large room in the Palace Hotel for two years before the Opera House facility was made available in 1903.

The Green's last two children, Richard and Ruth, were born in the hotel.

Richard Green died in 1906. Finding life too lonely in that big hotel without her husband and now grown children, Mrs. Green put the Palace up for sale.

The hotel was purchased for $3,000 in gold in 1911 by Joe and Anna Vergolio after they closed their saloon on First Street. Their grandaughter, Mary Tappero Mora, was born in the hotel five years later. During their second year of ownership, as their general store was still in business, the Vergolios leased the hotel to a couple.

For years there has been a story rumored around Cerrillos about two sisters who mysteriously disappeared after managing the Palace Hotel for a short time. In truth, this was the couple, assumed now to have been man and wife, who leased the hotel from the Vergolios in about 1912. Shortly after the couple took over, they bought a player piano, made one payment, gathered up most the hotel linens, and simply disappeared from Cerrillos, leaving the Vergolios with piano payments to take over and sheetless beds. (The player piano is still in the possession of Vergolio family members and bears a stamp showing the year 1912.)

The Vergolios managed to keep the hotel going during the succeeding years, but as the town became less of an attraction for visitors, they gradually closed off portions of the now 32-room hotel. Local carpenters and painters were kept busy through the years by the Vergolios who at one time had to have the entire roof replaced. By the 1940s the Vergolios's ages and the lack of business forced them to leave the care of the hotel to one or two more-or-less permanent residents.

Henry and Nellie Trigg bought the hotel from Anna Vergolio after Joe's death in 1947 and renamed it the Rock House Ranch. Their hotel, however, went the way of many businesses in Cerrillos after the railroad stop there had been discontinued, and eventually was closed to the public for many years.

The last proprietors were hotel residents Hank and Stephanie Salkheld who reopened the Palace in December 1965. When their management terminated, the hotel was taken over by a corporation. Then on 27 October 1968 the famous Palace Hotel was consumed by fire, leaving a bleak spot in the memories of many old timers.

Palace Hotel, after fire

Block 9 — Main Street Side

This was the block which was the site of the 1890 fire, and extended east and west from First to Second Streets, north and south from Railroad Avenue to Main Street. As most of the property owners had been insured at the time of the fire, businesses did not take long to reappear.

On the Main Street side at the corner of First in the early 1920s was a small cafe which served at times as the local gambling hall. This (or perhaps the Palace Hotel) was the site of the usual gambling card game with an unusual ending.

> *One of the players decided he was being dealt a crooked hand and accused the dealer. The dealer declared "no man can call me a cheat and live." The player was faster on the draw, however. The bullet meant for the dealer not only met its mark, but continued on through the dealer to penetrate the chest of the man seated behind him. The second man took a few more days to die from the second-hand shot.*

Next to the cafe was the location of one of the post offices, behind which was a bakery owned by Ross and Elizabeth Griffiths from about 1897 to the early 1900s. Built by George W. North after the 1890 fire, next was the North Building which extended from Railroad Avenue to Main Street. The Main Street section housed I.N. Stone's meat market in 1894. In 1897 it was occupied by F.H. Mitchell and his family where Mr. Mitchell ran the post office for the next three years. Later still it housed a barber shop, and in about 1915 was Mike Giraudo's dance hall.

Lot 9 Building remnants

Following those buildings were homes, including that of Mike Giraudo which he and his daughter built in later years. The establishment of the local undertaker was also in this block.

> *In the 1920s in one of the homes lived a close-knit family with about 12 children. This family was continuously the target of the goodwill of young Annie Giraudo who used to sneak food from her mother's cupboard for them. One of the children eventually went on to become a state senator.*

The opposite side of this block faced South Railroad Avenue and held several business establishments described later.

During the ensuing years as the buildings deteriorated and the adobe bricks from which some of them were constructed mysteriously disappeared, the business portion of the block remained vacant.

> *Somewhere in this area was the lot where, in the late 1890s, Cerrillos's baseball team, the Little Pittsburgs, played many a game against their stalwart opponents from Madrid and other surrounding communities.*

In the heydays of Cerrillos when brawls and shootings were almost an everyday occurrence, it was necessary to house the villainous apart from the villagers. The town jail, called the "lock up" on an 1893 map, was first situated in the middle of Main Street east of First near the old smelter. In 1894 the town council voted to move the jail to a location on Waldo Street east of First Street. How long the jail saw action is uncertain, as Cerrillos had a town Marshall for only a few years.

First Street, towards North

East side of First Street, going north from Main Street

On the northeast corner of First and Main Streets was a restaurant which a later owner turned into a ice cream parlor. (The post office was located in this building when Charles Lyon was postmaster in 1893.)

In 1918, Tony Tappero purchased that property from Ella Weltmer and replaced the existing structure with a new building. He then rented the building out to Fitte and Pete Sahd who set up Sahd Brothers Grocery Store which was quite successful for many years. In 1931 Pete Sahd left Cerrillos to open a grocery store in Taos. Fitte Sahd remained in business at this site until his death in 1939.

Cerrillos Bar

It was at that time that Tony Tappero reclaimed his building, converting the store into the Cerrillos Bar. The bar was referred to as Tony's Place by the locals.

His wife, Catarina, played an active part in managing the bar. In addition she was the community's early Avon distributor, and often walked the three miles to Madrid to sell Avon products.

After Catarina's death in 1965, Tony continued to maintain the bar alone until his own health started to fail. His daughter Mary and her husband, Leo Mora, moved from their home in Albuquerque to help her father in the management of the bar. The Moras continued to maintain the bar after Mr. Tappero's death in 1977.

On the back half of the next two lots was a two-story ice house and livery stable. In later years, in competition with three other dance halls, the area contained a dance hall pavilion.

The three lots from there to the corner of First and South Railroad contained, at one time or another, a laundry, a saloon, a grocery store, and a restaurant.

First Street was the original entry road to Cerrillos from the north. On this road still farther north of Cerrillos was a side road which led to the old Cerrillos Cemetery. A second cemetery nearby was established in later years for the town's Catholic population.

The AT&SF water tower was on the north side of the tracks at First Street, and the railroad station building was just east of the water tower.

In the early 1880s, the smelter and reduction works were located between the railroad tracks and the river at the east end of the village. This site was behind the buildings which later housed the Simoni Store (described later), and the Cerrillos Bar. In November 1897, after the river changed its course, a new 50-ton smelter was erected by the Mary Mining & Smelting Company on the hill northwest of town across the San Marcos arroyo. The property was deeded to the smelting company by the landowner, then Senator Stephen B. Elkins. Some remnants of this smelter survived through the years.

North Railroad Avenue

Along North Railroad Avenue in the early 1900s were a lumber office, a feed store, the usual saloon, a liquor warehouse, a photographer's shop, and a livery stable.

Cerrillos's first school, in 1883, was located on this side of the railroad tracks at Second and Richards Streets.

To Waldo, New Mexico

Continuing west on North Railroad Avenue, the road paralleled the railroad tracks, went past Devils's Throne, and finally reached the village of Waldo. Devil's Throne was a large rock formation which stood in the way

Devil's Throne

of the road as well as railroad property. In about 1944, a crew of local residents was hired by the railroad company to blast this rock. The road that resulted left much to be desired as far as driving comfort was concerned.

After the road left Waldo, it departed from the railroad tracks, traced old wagon trails and hidden mine claims until at last it met the main highway that runs between Santa Fe and Albuquerque.

With the closing of the Madrid coal mines in the 1950s came the demise of Waldo. The once frequently-used road from Cerrillos is now a series of bumps and hollows through the arroyo, past unrecognizable ruins of the old town of Waldo, finally reaching the main highway.

Like Cerrillos, Waldo had high hopes of growth, as it was at the end of the spur line from the Madrid coal mines. Apparently county planners also looked forward to the continued development of this town as, until as recently as 1986, a proud sign at Exit 267 on Highway 25 pointed the direction to the town of Waldo, New Mexico!

South Railroad Avenue, from First Street
Block 9 — Railroad Avenue Side

It was not long after the devasting fire of June 1890 that businesses were rebuilt on this side of the block on South Railroad Avenue between First and Second Streets. Torriano's Bar was at the corner of First Street, followed by two more saloons. Next door was the Griffiths' bakery which Mr.

Torianno's Bar, from left to right: Edith Torriano, Julia Vergolio, Elia Torriano, Lodie Torriano, Mary Torriano, Geneviene Vergolio, Emma (Simoni) Montoya.

Torriano acquired in later years. As described earlier, George North's building extended from Main to Railroad Avenue. In 1898 when F.H. Mitchell's post office faced the Main Street side, the Mitchells lived in the Railroad Avenue portion of the building. On the property next to Mitchell's residence in the 1920s was Mike Giraudo's garage.

On the corner at the other end of this block was Dr. Joseph Richards's drug store building, believed to have been built by Dr. Richards shortly after the 1890 fire. This building eventually became another of Cerrillos's saloons.

> *One evening during the 1920-1930 prohibition period, the "madam"*
> *that ran the saloon became upset when an attempt to raid her establishment*
> *was made by two local constables. Her strenuous objection was emphasized*
> *as she shot through the door, injuring one of the men through his hand and the*
> *other through his knee. It is unlikely that the attempted raid was successful.*

In 1968 the newly-established volunteer fire department occupied the building and used it to house one of their fire trucks. The fire department vacated this building when their new garage was built in 1979, but the building continued for several years to be known as the "fire house building." Later that year, the owner donated the building for use by the Cerrillos Health Clinic until their new facility was completed the following year.

Fire House Building

On South Railroad Avenue across Second Street on the corner was the office of the *Rustler*. Next to that was D.D. Harkness's Cerrillos House Hotel built in 1880. Both survived the fire of 1890.

In later years from at least 1894 to 1898, J.P. McFadean acquired the Cerrillos House and called the new establishment the Hotel Mac. (In 1892, it is believed to have been the San Pedro Hotel, owned by Mr. Valentine Schick and managed by Mr. McFadean.) Private residences followed the Cerrillos House.

> *At one of the little houses, one evening a gentleman caller knocked on the front door of the home of his lady friend. Spurning the continuation of their affair, as she was married, she refused to open the door. The gentleman proceeded to shoot her through the glass door. This act undoubtedly discouraged her from further extramarital frolicking!*
>
> *Some time later in this same house, a man — possibly the husband of the wandering wife — came home drunk and decided to have it out with his mother-in-law. After much protest, more than likely, she went along with him on a walk along the railroad tracks. What provoked his anger towards her is uncertain. At any rate, he pulled out a knife and ended the life of his mother-in-law.*

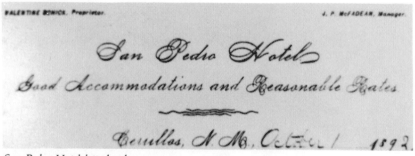

San Pedro Hotel letterhead

In this block also was the printing and telegraph office, which were later moved across Railroad Avenue, followed by a stage depot, then a carpenter shop and a lumber yard.

In September 1897, "Judge" Austin L. Kendall purchased the plot of land extending from Third Street back to the arroyo, lying between South Railroad Avenue and Main Street. He sold a small portion of his property to F.H. Mitchell, and built a residence for himself on the remainder of the lot. Kendall served as the Justice of the Peace in Cerrillos from April 1895 to January 1901, which probably accounted for his title as Judge.

East side of First Street, north from Main Street

Returning to the starting point at First Street and Main, across from the Tiffany Saloon the building on the southeast corner was owned by clothier J.H. Gerdes in the early 1890s. Developing into a general store and then a saloon, the owners were Tom DeLallo in the early 1900s, then Mike Leyba. Phil Sandoval ran the store for DeLallo for many years. One of the owners added the unique pointed false front to distinguish it from other saloons in Cerrillos.

In 1934, Tony Simoni purchased that corner saloon building from Mr. Leyba. It later became the Monte Carlo Bar, then Mitchell's Antique Store, then later the Jericho Store.

The two-story building next to that building was purchased in 1918 by Mr. Simoni from E.W. Callender.

Monte Carlo Bar

The Simoni Store

The upper story of this building was a lodging (boarding) house, and a balcony ran across the entire front of the building. One half of the first floor held a grocery and general merchandise store. The other half was primarily a feed store. An early sign indicated "A. Simoni-Probst Merchandise." August Probst was a Cerrillos resident whose meat market was probably at that location.

39

Simoni Store, original

The one-story building on the other side of the Simoni Store was leased by the Tiffany owners in the 1970s for their Starlight Cabaret.

A two-lot building next to that, going towards Waldo Street, was Joe Granito's general store. In the early 1920s he leased the store to the Sahd Brothers, Pete and Fitte.

The businesses in the remainder of that block were also owned by Joe Granito: A dance hall/theater, and a garage.

> In the 1920s the dance hall building was used for various community events, one memorial occasion being the wedding dance of a Cerrillos couple. Unfortunately, the bridegroom decided to dance at his own wedding with another married woman whom he had been seeing on the sly. Her husband, very upset over this display of boldness, objected and told the new bridgroom, "I'll get you for this!"
>
> The next day they prepared for their honeymoon. The groom was leaving DeLallo's general store on the corner (with a corset for his bride under his arm) as the deceived husband waited between the buildings, gun in hand. Without warning, he shot and killed the new bridegroom, thus ending a marriage before it began.

It was in this area, around the corner on Waldo Street, that the town jail was relocated in 1894.

The lots across Waldo on First Street, beginning at the corner of Waldo, were uninhabitable for many years until the Galisteo River finally changed its course. This section of the block was the site of the road that led to the first bridge across the arroyo. Cerrillos's first Catholic Church was located on the adjacent lots towards River Street.

Iglesia de San Jose (St. Joseph's Church)

Prior to 1881, Cerrillos's Catholic community was served by a visiting priest from Pena Blanca. From 1881 to 1918, a priest from Our Lady of Guadalupe Parish in Santa Fe serviced the area. Then in 1918, Cerrillos was transferred back to the care of the Pena Blanca Franciscan Fathers. At that time the church building was located in the lot next to its present site.

Then in 1922, the new St. Joseph's Catholic Church was built by a local crew of carpenters headed by Frank Schmitt. A Franciscan from Pena Blanca, Father Jerome Hesse, was the first pastor. The pastor's residence next door was built later in the 1920s on the lot where the old church had been located.

In 1939 Cerrillos was made into a Parish, at which time the priest was Rev. Eugene Rousseau. During the years 1939 to 1959, eleven priests were assigned to Cerrillos, serving one to four years.

Cerrillos saw good fortune when, in 1960, Fray Angelico Chavez became priest of the church.

Fray Chavez's contributions to the literary world is extensive and includes fiction and non-fiction novels, poetry, and literature commentaries. The October 1960 issue of the Catholic Digest featured him as "Poet in a Ghost Town," a brief story of his life and current, at that time, experience in Cerrillos.

While pastoring in Cerrillos, Fray Chavez undertook the restoration of the St. Francis Church in Golden, New Mexico. He remained priest of St. Joseph's Church in Cerrillos for about five years, but the severe winters forced him to request transfer to a milder climate in Albuquerque in 1964.

Following Fray Chavez's tenure at St. Joseph's, Reverend Giles Hukenbeck served from 1965 until 1972 when Father Otto Krische was assigned to the Cerrillos Parish.

Father Otto Krische

Father Otto Krische had served in Wichita, Kansas from 1950 to 1955; in Clovis, New Mexico from 1956 to 1963; and in Pena Blanca from 1964 to 1973, before being assigned to Cerrillos at St. Joseph's Catholic Church (Iglesia de San Jose). Father Otto, as he is affectionately known by the parishioners, has added a garage and a workshop to the priest's home since his arrival. Although Father Otto and Cerrillos have been good for each other, he admits that the time for his retirement is approaching. What better place than in Cerrillos.

St. Joseph's Church

Down Waldo Street

As described earlier, a meat market and shoe store was on the corner of Waldo and First Street at the end of the block from the Tiffany Saloon. Down Waldo at Second Street was Rosendo Ortiz's grocery store where he was in business from about 1927 to the early 1960s.

The remains of a small adobe structure, which was built before 1902, still stands on property across the street on Waldo.

Further down on Waldo, between Third Street and the arroyo was the Methodist Episcopal Church. The property was purchased from Stephen Elkins by W.C. Hurt, trustee for the church, in January 1884. The church itself, an adobe structure, was built during 1884 and 1885 by its pastor for the first two years, W.B. Wheeler. There was a parsonage for the church reported in church statistics in 1893. The church property was sold to H.C. Kinsell in Jaunary 1896. Services there, however, continued until sometime after 1907.

At one time, the road to the town of Waldo, New Mexico, ran behind the church, through the arroyo, and crossed the railroad tracks at Waldo. Across

Adobe shed

the road from the church were the back lots of the Palace Hotel. While Joe Vergolio was the owner of the Palace, those lots held orchards of about 100 grapevines and fruit trees.

After Third, the cross streets — Railroad, Main, Waldo, and River — ended abruptly at the rim of the Galisteo Arroyo. One wonders how many unstable souls have been surprised by the long step down from those streets after a Saturday night spree!

Although streets, buildings, houses, businesses, and some individuals have been described, one's imagination must come into play when trying to feel the excitement, heartbreak, success, and tragedy for the hundreds of people who moved into, passed through, or left from Cerrillos. The once-lively boom town saw its share of Saturday night brawls, Sunday picnics, Fourth of July celebrations. Imagine the looks of hopeful anticipation of passengers getting off at the train station; the disappointed and broke prospector sneaking into the boxcar trying to get out of town; the laughter of children when school was out. Imagine, if you can, cattle making their way down the middle of the village streets; then later horse-drawn wagons; and finally, the automobiles causing dust to fly as people and horses got out of their way.

IV. ALMOST A GHOST TOWN

What did happen to cause the near demise of Cerrillos, New Mexico?

Members of the old families that have remained recall those days when most all of the townsfolk knew and relied on each other. They tell about the church, their school days, the dance halls, the theater. There are gaps in their memories, however, probably because some remember only what they want to recall — the good times; and the newer residents only know what they have heard. The old timers who knew about the town before it started to fade away are either no longer around or prefer to cherish the old memories in the privacy of their hearts.

Cerrillos was a town dependent upon the continuous wealth brought in from the nearby mines and the railroad. Even before the turn of the century, however, this wealth was starting to dwindle. As the mines became less productive, some miners and their families had to leave the area and try to survive elsewhere by other means.

The coal mines of Madrid were affected by the loss of miners to the wartime jobs in shipbuilding, munitions plants, and the armed services during World War II. Even more so, the introduction to the railroad of diesel fuel ended the usefulness of coal. All these things caused the eventual abandonment of Waldo and nearly the end of Madrid and Cerrillos. Madrid managed to hold its own, probably because of its location directly on the highway and subsequent open exposure to tourists.

Businessmen began to close their shops as customers moved away, and the old buildings of Cerrillos crumbled with age.

Profitable turquoise findings in the immediate area of Mt. Chalchihuitl dwindled in the early 1900s. In earlier years, between 1885 and 1891, persistent pursuers had located another area of turquoise-producing hills about three miles northeast of the original lode. In 1892, in this area known as Turquoise Hills, the new holdings were purchased by the American Turquoise Company in which the Tiffany Company of New York had a principal interest. The larger of these claims was labeled the "Tiffany," the other being the Castillian. Production from these claims was quite profitable for the American Turquoise Company through about 1899 when further extensive exploration was lessened.

By 1902, the population of Cerrillos, which had peaked at about 2,500 in 1890, was now down to less than 500. The actual voting population in town was many times less than that size.

In October 1903, the town marshall was discharged, as the town no longer had a justice of the peace. On February 11, 1904, an official vote of twenty-three residents for and eight against resulted in disincorporation of the town of Cerrillos. The Town Council held its final meeting on March 19, 1904. The last entry in the minutes of that meeting stated: "A motion made to adjourn for good. Carried, I guess," somewhat symbolizing the sentiments of the old timers. It was signed by Jose S. Gonzales, Clerk.

Then in 1907 there was an air of hope about the town. An optimistic writer for the *Santa Fe New Mexian Daily* (who was also a property owner in Cerrillos) indicated that there continued to be an influx of people because of continuous work on properties (turquoise mines) in the Los Cerrillos district by Denver mining men. He further reported that people were still looking for houses to live in, as "there is no vacant house" in Cerrillos.

Some work in the area of the Tiffany and Castillian mines did continue through the years. Hopes for revival of Cerrillos were short-lived, however, as this new drive towards mining riches was halted in about 1920.

Of the other original large mines in the area, only the Ortiz mine really survived. Employing over sixty residents in as recently as 1986, the mining operation at the Ortiz gradually faded until it was finally abandoned in 1987. With the closing of this mine, more families were forced to leave Cerrillos to seek other means of survival.

Railroad Station Building

The railroad station closed in the 1940s when the railroad converted to diesel fuel and no longer depended upon the coal supplied in the Cerrillos area. Madrid coal mines were abandoned in the 1950s. The Cerrillos railroad station building was moved in the 1950s to Estancia Valley southeast of Cerrillos.

Because of potenial danger, the top story of the school across the arroyo had been condemned in 1943 and had to be removed. The high school students, therefore, had to transfer to other schools, leaving only grade school students in attendance. During the 1957-1959 school year there were three teachers for the approximately 70 students. As families left the area, the school population lessened so that eventually grades five through eight were eliminated from the school. Finally at the end of the 1961-1962 school year, Cerrillos Elementary School closed, and the precinct became part of

School, with classes

the Santa Fe County school district. The interior of the vacant brick school was consumed by fire in the 1970s, leaving a skeleton of memories for children and adults as well.

Thus, Cerrillos was well on its way to becoming a real ghost town.

School skeleton

V. SURVIVORS AND REVIVERS

Movies

Cerrillos's beginnings were the result of the migration of prospectors, miners, and businessmen from the far reaches of the United States, and even beyond. So, it seemed only natural that its revival would be dependent upon outsiders.

The town's fading buildings had been used as early as the mid-1940s as backgrounds for movies. However, such ventures had little positive affect on the village until 1958. It was then that the Walt Disney studios from Hollywood, California, saw in the town the perfect setting for western films, with its dirt streets, board sidewalks, and typical old west storefronts. Portions of the television series, *Nine Lives of Elfego Baca,* were filmed in Cerrillos during that year. The re-opening of the Tiffany Saloon in 1962 helped to keep Cerrillos alive after the Elfego Baca series was completed.

In 1968 Disney again used Cerrillos streets for the filming of *Pancho,* and in 1971 for the television series, *The Bear Cats,* A Lone Ranger movie was filmed in Cerrillos in May 1980 as was a portion of *The Ballad of Gregorio Cortez* in 1982. More recently, in May 1986, Cerrillos's First Street was the background for scenes of *Outrageous Fortune,* featuring Bette Midler, Shelly Long, Peter Coyote, and George Carlin.

During such filmings probably the most unusual sight were the policemen that stood in the middle of the road at First and Main Streets directing Cerrillos traffic!

Newspapers

The *Rustler* newspaper was revived in 1978, published by "The Concerned Citizens of Cerrillos, Inc." Editors were Marc Schneider, Ross Lockridge, and Paula Sherman. Some frequent contributors were Emma Montoya, Josie Anaya, Chips Woodruff, Lourdes Lucero, and Mildred Beach. Although the new version was rather short-lived and was terminated sometime around 1980, it did give the communities of Cerrillos and Madrid a boost during its publication period.

The newest endeavor is the semimonthly *East Mountain Telegraph* which began publication in January 1988 from Tijeras, New Mexico. Cerrillos was featured in at least three of its issues in the first three months of publication.

Fiesta de la Primavera

Early in 1968 the area in and around Cerrillos experienced a series of property-devastating fires which convinced the citizens of the need for more localized fire-fighting capabilities.

As a result of a series of meetings led by H.D. "Chips" Woodruff of the nearby Turquoise Six Ranch, a major fund-raising event was planned for the purchase of equipment. This first fiesta was held in June 1968.

It was such a success that the following year the Fiesta de la Primavera

Fiesta crowd

was launched as an annual event. Sponsored by the Turquoise Trail Volunteer Fire Department each year, the Fiesta has attracted thousands of visitors and has been a great social event for the community as well as a fund-raiser for businesses.

The opening parade features the fire department vehicles, the Santa Fe Fiesta queen, homemade floats, Shriners, and cowboys. Activities and attractions include booths selling native cusine, jewelry, other arts and crafts, dance demonstrations and a street dance. The Fiesta is highlighted by a water hosing contest between the local volunteer fire departments. The 1979 Fiesta celebrated the town's 100th anniversary.

The participation in the 1986 and 1987 Fiesta de la Primavera was not as great as it had been in prior years, because the county imposed unexpected additional taxes for the entertainment and amusement acitivities usually offered. Even with such obstacles, the Fiesta will undoubtedly continue to be celebrated each year. The year 1989 will mark the twentieth anniversary of this affair as an annual event as well as the 110th birthday of the village of Ceriillos.

Fiesta water hose fight

Turquoise Trail Volunteer Fire Department

With the financial success of the Fiesta in 1968, Chips Woodruff's dream of the development of a volunteer fire department was well underway. They were able to purchase two trucks for the department in time for that first Fiesta.

The Turquoise Trail Volunteer Fire Department (TTVFD) was officially established at their first formal meeting which was held in Tony Tappero's Cerrillos Bar. In Mr. Tappero's honor, they continue to hold their annual meeting and election of officers in the Cerrillos Bar on the corner of First and Main Streets.

The once vacant lot on River Street diagonally across from the priest's home at the corner of First and Waldo Streets is the site of the TTVFD Station No. 1 which houses their vehicles. Built in 1979, the building was dedicated to the TTVFD's founder, H.D. Woodruff. During the annual Fiesta while the fire trucks are on exhibit in the parade, the empty fire station is the Fiesta food center, serving native dishes as well as the usual hamburgers and hot dogs to hungry patrons.

TTVFD Building

TTVFD Building, Food Bar

Health Clinic

In June 1979, the *Rustler* had reported that for the past year the Cerrillos-Madrid Clinic had been located in the basement of the home of John Aragon. The staff continued to look for a more permanent home for the Clinic.

After the Volunteer Fire Department vacated the premises on Railroad Avenue, the owner donated that building to the Health Clinic in August 1979.

Then in April 1980, a building was constructed on Waldo Street next to the church for the Health Clinic as well as for the veterinarian who made regular visits to attend to the area's pets.

Cerrillos soon outgrew this structure, and early in 1987 it was replaced by a more substantial Parish Hall. It not only accommodates the Health Clinic, but also provides a community hall for the use of all residents.

Health Clinic, old

Health Clinic, new

State Highway Department

Although the streets of Cerrillos remain unpaved, the residents have a big advantage over even larger communities: Their community is the center of operations for the State Highway Department's maintenance vehicles for Highway 14 and other roads in the surrounding area!

Tiffany Saloon Grounds

Fortunately, the fire of March 1977 which resulted in the end of the Tiffany Saloon did not reach the living quarters of the owners, Nadine Heiden and Fran Eckols. Their next two years were difficult, to say the least, as Miss Heiden and Miss Eckols attempted to put their lives back together through the chaos and ruin of their dream. In the spring of 1979, with the help of local residents, they buried the past, filling in the collapsed section of the old building, rebuilding the adobe walls surrounding the property, and repairing the weakened building walls and roof. Through the next few years, they spent hours in the refurbishing of their home and working in the gardens and courtyard, resulting in a comfortable residence behind the adobe walls.

Then in 1986 a fatal illness struck Nadine Heiden, resulting in her untimely death that year. Fran Eckols has continued to live in their home in Cerrillos, remaining in contact with many of the celebrities that came through the door of their once world renowned Tiffany.

Tiffany adobe walls

The Plaza

The lots located between Railroad Avenue and Main Street, across from the Tiffany Saloon grounds, had been consumed by fire in 1890. Burned building skeletons were soon replaced by new business houses. Those buildings, however, went the way of many Cerrillos structures during the ensuing years as they were abandoned. Materials from which they had been built either rotted away or were carted off to be used elsewhere. The lot was left vacant, but unsightly for years.

In the summer of 1968, the citizens of Cerrillos got together to clean this lot of the debris accumulated during the years. Under the leadership of the Joe Luceros, they planted pounds of grass seed and hundreds of flowering plants. Nadine Heiden and Fran Eckols, owners of the Tiffany across the street, had a gazebo built over the area where the oven of the old bakery had been located.

Still vacant except for the blue-topped gazebo in the center, this lot was Cerrillos' Plaza (NOTE: During the 1988 filming of *Young Guns*, the gazebo was removed.) On sunny weekend days, residents as well as tourists could be found picknicking, tossing frisbies, playing ball, or just sitting and watching the world go by. On the weekend evenings, however, the serenity of the quiet community was often disturbed by a more lively group of park users.

Whether the Plaza should remain in its park-like setting, become a commerical development, or be sold to a home builder will depend upon the direction of enthusiasm of Cerrillos residents in addition to, of course, the desires of the current owners of the plaza property.

Plaza; gazebo

Cerrillos Cafe Building

The old Cerrillos Cafe at the corner of Main and Second Streets has sometimes been reopened by the various owners during the Fiesta de la Primavera. Purchased in about 1960 by Joe Sahd whose family owned the remainder of the lots on Second Street, it had been leased by several individuals through the years. Each tried his or her hand at making this much-needed business a success, but for some reason the endeavors were short-lived. Built before the turn of the century, the building remains one of the town's old landmarks.

Cerrillos Cafe

Kludgit Sound, Inc. (Opera House Building)

In 1979 the Los Cerrillos mining district was nominated for listing in the National Register of Historic Places. Because of objections by a few of the property owners, this nomination was unsuccessful. The Opera House of Cerrillos, however, was approved for listing on the State Register of Cultural Properties in March 1974 after nomination by Marc Simmons.

The building, located on Main between Second and Third Streets, is still standing, its exterior having changed little during the years since the 1974 nomination. In 1977 the property was purchased by an enterprising recording engineer, Baird Banner, for his Kludgit Sound, Inc., recording studio. Although it was a seemingly impossible endeavor, Mr. Banner built an accoustically-correct studio within the frame of the old stone building.

Mr. Banner's clients for 24-track recording sessions have been primarily New Mexico, Texas, and California artists, but have also included a variety of motion pictures, most recently *The Milagro Beanfield War*.

The seclusion of the village apparently appeals to musicians who could give their all in relaxed surroundings.

Opera House

Palace Hotel Grounds

On the lot on which the Palace Hotel stood so regally in its day can be found one remaining corner of the old building. Some of the stone from the building was used to support the tower of the "Tower House" located two blocks away. The lot itself was for a brief time occupied by llamas. Having faith in the possiblities of a new business enterprise, their owners brought the llamas to Cerrillos and utilized them for tourist pack trips into the surrounding mine areas. The llamas were indeed a featured attraction during visits of tourists to this town.

Palace Hotel grounds

The Cerrillos Bar

Leo and Mary Tappero Mora still keep their Cerrillos Bar open for more or less regular hours, but do not hesitate to close up if things appear to be getting rowdy. Their daughter, Kathy, is living in Albuquerque with her daughter, Tammy, the Moras' only grandchild. The bar is located at First and Main Streets, and the Moras insist it will remain a family business and are looking forward to their time of retirement.

In addition to the bar, the Moras maintain the town's only gas (Regular) pump.

The bar stocks the usual saloon "spirits" for consumption mainly by tourists. Stacked against the back wall, however, are cases of soda and beer which are the mainstay of the residents as well as the prospectors who have come down from the hills for a day of people mixing.

This is a social gathering place for townsfolks as well as visitors. Today one can almost always find a challenger waiting around to join in a game of pool at the bar's main attraction.

Cerrillos Bar

"Emma's Building"

Upon Tony Simoni's death in 1956, the building at the corner of First and Main was left to his daughter, Emma, and her husband, Eugene Montoya. In 1980 it was occupied by Dale Kruse as The Pure Wood (art) Gallery. Concurrently, the staff of the revived *Rustler* newspaper maintained an office in the building.

During the years, Gene and Emma Montoya preferred to keep their building available for community use. It continues to be used to display art work during the Fiesta, and at one time or another housed wedding receptions and birthday parties, and has been used as a meeting place when the need arose.

In addition to its pointed false front, for years the building could be recognized by the words "La Cantanita," the name used for a Disney film, across the front window.

"Emma's Building" /Simoni Store

The Simoni Store

The Simoni Store has been run by Edith and Corrina Simoni since their father's death in 1956. The store is a museum of remembrances of the "old days" — some for sale and some just to look at: toys, ceramics, jewelry and novelties made by local craftspeople. Ice cream, candy, soda and beer are also for sale, and modern computer game machines are reminders of the age we are living in.

The three sisters (Emma lives next door) are rarely at a loss for lively, upbeat conversation. They are always ready to explain the display of newspaper articles about old Cerrillos and photographs of their family and of movies made there.

The boarding house rooms upstairs from the store are closed to the public as they are part of the Simonis' living quarters.

The What-Not Shop

Three of the lots on First Street down from the Cerrillos Bar are now occupied by one of the town's antique stores. E.J. (Mitch) and Margie Mitchell, residents since about 1954, take great pride in their What-Not Shop which, like many of the buildings in Cerrillos, went through stages of various businesses before the Mitchells took over.

The old flour and grain bins used when the building held a grocery store still exist behind one of the counters. The Mitchells also possess a cash register rescued from Emma Montoya's building where their first antique shop was located. The label on the cash register shows it was built 19 March 1905.

In front of the What-Not Shop stands Cerrillos's only public telephones.

As the name suggests, their shop contains everything from native-made jewelry to antique china; from old postcards to railroad track studs; from pottery to lanterns. Thus, the Mitchell's widely-advertised What-Not Shop is more like a museum than an antique store, and one can find many relics of the past of Cerrillos and the surrounding area. The Shop is advertised by the American Automobile Association in the New Mexico edition of their monthly publication.

What-Not Shop

The Old Boarding House

The block-long (and wide) estate on Third Street and South Railroad Avenue is called "The Old Boarding House" by its owners since 1967, Jim and Patra Smith. The original owner, Austin Kendall, sold the property to Juanita de Olivas, who in turn sold it to Edgar and Elizabeth Andrews.

The house once served as a boarding house under Mrs. Andrews's ownership, and part of the building accommodated the Pure Food grocery store. At one time under the present ownership it was known as the "Old Boarding House Museum and Antique Shop." The original structure is still a part of the present house.

The Smiths' introduction to Cerrillos was through a chance visit to the Tiffany Restaurant after attending the funeral of her son in Santa Fe in 1967. The old boarding house they saw down the street from the Palace Hotel had been empty for about six years. Taking on the task of clearing out the yard of debris and restoring the building appeared to the Smiths as a means of working off their sorrow at that time.

The buildings and gardens beautifully maintained by the Smiths have turned the property into a show place for tourists as well as an island of contentment for the Smiths.

Old Boarding House

Adobe Antiques

On two of the lots originally owned by Joe Granito, which follow the Simoni property, now stands Adobe Antiques, built in 1975 by Claude and Mary Jobe, both retired school teachers. The Jobes "discovered" Cerrillos during a vacation trip to Santa Fe from their home in California. While dining at Tiffanys, their attention was drawn to a lot in the next block, vacant except for a trailer house. They envisioned that spot as an ideal place for their retirement venture.

In addition to displaying authentic antiques in their shop, Mary Jobe is further able to share her knowledge of antiques in her writings as a columnist for *Santa Fe Lifestyle Magazine* on various collectibles.

Adobe Antiques

Casa Grande Trading Post

Todd and Patricia Brown, with their six children, have been in the Cerrillos area since about 1970. They built their 20-room adobe home, located at Waldo and Third Streets, on the Palace Hotel property. It faces the site of the old Methodist Church and overlooks both the Galisteo and the San Marcos Arroyos.

The Brown's Casa Grande Trading Post and Turquoise Museum at the end of Waldo Street contains, among other items, turquoise, silver, and shell jewelry from the Santo Domingo Pueblo, and native clothing for sale, as well as displaying gemstones, rocks, and arrowheads of the area.

Their adjoining Petting Zoo is a tourist attraction with its goats, ducks, chickens, and a donkey who thinks he is a dog. The Browns give tours of old mines and gold panning on request, and also have bed-and-breakfast accommodations for tourists.

Casa Grande

Rancho San Marcos

The lots at First Street and North Railroad Avenue are now occupied by the Rancho San Marcos antique store. The adobe structure is surrounded by a coyote fence which lends an air of mystery to its contents. Most notable exhibits are the owner's display of mining and railroad relics. Rancho San Marcos is currently being run by Fred Montoya, a native of Cerrillos.

Rancho San Marcos

Post Office

On the corner of south Waldo at Third Street is perhaps the village's most frequented business, the U.S. Post Office. Cerrillos-born Alice Lopez has been postmaster for more than twenty-five years, over twenty years at this same site when the post office building was constructed. Alice's parents, Brijido and Piedad Montoya came to Cerrillos in 1926. Her father has since passed away, but Piedad still lives in the village a block or so away from the Post Office.

Post Office

"Otro Lado"

On the other side of the arroyo south of metropolitan Cerrillos, the residents are very much a part of the community.

After the school across the arroyo was closed down in the 1960s, the property was purchased by a mural artist, as the sturdy gymnasium appeared ideal for his type of endeavor. Setting up a residence in the remains of the school building itself, however, proved to be unwise, as it soon became another Cerrillos victim of fire.

The property was then sold in 1987 to a sculptor from Arizona. He is utilizing the sturdy gymnasium as a workshop while his artwork is being displayed in other parts of the southwest. Surrounded by a white-painted cement enclosure, the old school, the gymnasium building and grounds make an impressive sight as seen from the highway just before the entry road to Cerrillos.

George Borque moved to Cerrillos in about 1972 where he produced his photographs of Cerrillos and the surrounding areas under his business name *Bullfrog Eclipse*. In addition to photography, he is perhaps better known as a musician, having played with the group, Last Mile Ramblers, from 1973 for eleven years. While they were not on tour or making albums, the Ramblers' Blue Grass music was shared with the community every Sunday at the Golden Inn in Golden, New Mexico.

Another recent resident musician is currently based in Silverton, Colorado, although he still has a home in Cerrillos.

The other side also boasts of a day care center, and one of the residents is a construction contractor who is currently building a new house in that section of the village.

Sculptor's building

VI. NEW BUSINESS VENTURES

New business enterprises have recently made their appearance in Cerrillos.

An attractive adobe structure facing River Street at the end of Third is called the Tower House by residents. Three feet of the tower base were built of the stone from the Palace Hotel ruins. The current owner of the Tower House, Mary Lynn Comeau, opened up a shop in her home in 1987 displaying her talents as a fiber artist and designer. Ms. Comeau's *Makara-Three Rivers Flowing* gallery specializes in contemporary ethnic apparel and accessories primarily with a southwestern influence. Already, her designs have been featured in shops from coast to coast.

Tower House

Cerrillos has a Ph.D. in its midst, Jo Sage. Dr. Sage owns the home at the end of Waldo located on the site of the old Methodist Church. Because of its unusual shape, the house is sometimes referred to as the "snail house." Dr. Sage is an instructor of meditation using light energies for accelerated conscious spiritual growth. The serenity of the Cerrillos area appears to be ideal for her teachings and she has classes in Santa Fe as well as in Cerrillos.

In addition to her teaching. Dr. Sage operates an unadvertised bed-and-breakfast arrangment in her home which has already been utilized by Cerrillos residents for visiting family members.

Across Railroad Avenue at the bend of the road on First Street is Ray Perguidi's *Cerrillos Hair Shop and Special Effects.* Mr. Perguidi discovered

Cerrillos about five years ago when he decided to try Highway 14 from Albuquerque to visit his sister in Santa Fe. Finding that road spiritually uplifting, he stopped at various roadside areas, Mile Marker 129, then Golden, Madrid, and finally off the main road to Cerrillos. After commuting from Albuquerque to his job in Santa Fe for two or three months, Mr. Perguidi tired of the long ride and the "big city." Finally in September 1987 he found what he was looking for in the serenity of Cerrillos.

Ray had spent most of his adult life in the field of cosmetology, working with the "stars" and other celebrities from Hollywood to New York looking for that big break. In Albuquerque he had worked with the Classic Theater Company, the Albuquerque Opera, and the Civic Light Opera hoping to make the right contacts, but to no avail; and that type of volunteer work became tiring and disappointing.

What is ironic is that it took a move to the obscure village of Cerrillos for his talents to finally be discovered. It was here that Hollywood found him during the 1988 filming of *Young Guns*. Ray was hired immediately and continued to work with that movie to the last day of shooting. In addition, he has become involved in the New Mexico Film Commission for contacts with future Cerrillos area films.

Ray is elated with his new life and his own shop in Cerrillos and has nothing but the highest praise for the area, the people he has met, and the future of this village.

One of Cerrillos's newer residents is David Michael Kennedy whose photographic successes are well known particularly in the New York area. Mr. Kennedy was a commercial photographer in New York for eighteen years, photographing celebrities, shooting record covers, major ad campaigns, and editorial work. Among his clients were Bob Dylan, Bruce Springsteen, and Julian Lennon. One of David's goals was to get away from the stress of commercial photography, find a peaceful place to settle, and promote his personal work.

About five years ago he and his wife, Lucy, found themselves traveling around the country and subsequently fell in love with the southwest area. About two years ago they started getting serious about making a move, and Santa Fe looked better and better. Mr. Kennedy was commissioned in Albuquerque to do photographs of Toney Anaya, after which they drove up Highway 14 toward Santa Fe. There was Madrid on the main highway, and off the road they discovered Cerrillos. There were people there, but this was a quiet, serene place out of the way. Here they decided to settle, moving into their home in the summer of 1987.

David gives much praise and credit to Lucy who has been his right arm and probably most critical and helpful advisor. Lucy does the matting and framing of David's photographs.

Although David Michael Kennedy has received many awards for his photography, his purpose in the Cerrillos area is for him and his family to relax and enjoy life in this quiet community and to share his own personal photographic works with others.

VII. NEARBY ATTRACTIONS

The Turquoise Hills Venture

A new type of prospector made a gallant attempt to revitalize the "little hills." The Turquoise Hills mining area about six miles north of Cerrillos was reopened in 1985 by an industrious venturer, Don Clark, who kept busy reclaiming cuttable gemstones from old tailings. Don's dream was to build the Turquoise Hills area into a public park where visitors could play prospector in the mounds of tailings Don wanted to open for that purpose.

The Turquoise Hills site has historical as well as archaeological significance which Mr. Clark felt could be better preserved if the area were made into a state park. A Turquoise Hill Monument Foundation was set up in the fall of 1987 to accept donations for this project. Unfortunately, the Foundation was unsuccessful in reaching its required monetary goal before the deadline set by the State of New Mexico.

Although the specific dreams of Don Clark will not be fulfilled, the site will be preserved. Early in 1988 that property and surrounding acreage was purchased by two Santa Fe jewelers who hope to produce turquoise to sell to crafts people and perhaps use in their own designs.

Rancho Viejo

About 8 miles north of Cerrillos, beginning above Highway 22, a 23,000 acre development under the name of Rancho Viejo is being envisioned by three businessmen. Long-range plans include private homes, apartments, a business park, and a shopping center.

A focus of this development is the Santa Fe Community College campus east of Richards Avenue about five miles south of the city limits. A few miles south of this area, across Highway 14 from the State Penitentiary is an area planned for the National Guard Armory. Still farther south is the San Marcos Subdivision. These sites as well as some acreage that are state trust lands are dispersed within the development acreage of Rancho Viejo. Several roads are proposed to extend from east Interstate 25 to west Interstate 25, crossing Highway 14.

Although only the college and the National Guard Armory are in the plan for the immediate future, such a development by Rancho Viejo could have a positive effect on property values in the Cerrillos area.

Pueblo Ruins

In late 1987 there was a recent disclosure of the existence of several unexcavated ancient pueblo ruins in and around the Cerrillos area. Most were located on privately-owned lands. One, however, was purchased in 1987 by an archaeological organization that preserves and studies such sites. This is the San Marcos Pueblo, located about 4 miles north of Cerrillos.

Excavators and other scientists doing research and field work in this pueblo would probably require temporary accommodations during their research. Where else but Cerrillos?

So it would appear that this obscure little village, once, according to rumor, favored as the New Mexico state capitol, refuses to die. Some old timers still believe in undisclosed riches to be found thereabouts; other old timers wistfully recall the way things were. Some of the more recent residents would like a little more activity in the community as long as the Cerrillos way of life is not adversely affected. Most all, however, are content with their sleepy little town as it is — as long as it can remain alive.

VIII. AND NOW . . .

Movies to the Rescue

In March 1988 there was indeed activity in this sleepy town of less than 250 residents. It was again invaded by Hollywood filmmakers who rediscovered its worth as a backdrop for western movies. The crew of a Billy The Kid epic called *Young Guns*, starring Emilio Estevez, Kiefer Sutherland, Charlie Sheen and Lou Diamond Phillips, took over Cerrillos and returned it, Hollywood-style, to its yesterdays.

Drooping false fronts of old buildings received face lifts, streets that had been packed solid by automobiles were redusted to give them the original dirt-street appearance, modern day improvements were hidden by false adobe walls.

Although the changes to the buildings, homes, and yards were meant to be temporary, some residents and business persons retained them as the changes enhance the appearance of their property. They also helped to give the town the boost it needed to entice the return of tourism and future film makers.

As in the past, many of the local residents were given parts as extras. Although this movie inconvenienced a few residents, the overall excitement and enthusiasm could be felt throughout the town during the few weeks of shooting. On the final Saturday, sightseers lined their cars on both sides of Main Street from First back to the highway; a few were fortunate enough to be able to drive into town during breaks in the filming and park along the streets in town.

Although movie making in Cerrillos is not new, this particular filming was timely. The grand opening of another New Mexico-made film in Santa Fe on that last weekend brought in celebrities and other tourists to Cerrillos that probably were not even aware of the little village's existence.

Once again, the movies came to the rescue of Cerrillos.

Water Problems Resolved

Back in April 1892, the Atchison, Topeka and Santa Fe (AT&SF) Railroad was asked to establish a water supply service for Cerrillos. As a result they built a dam and pipeline to furnish the railroad and the town with water from the San Marcos springs. As the years went by, various businessmen petitioned the Town Council for ordinances granting them the right to lay water pipe to their places of business. Because of continuous need in the town, the Cerrillos Water and Irrigation Company purchased water directly from the AT&SF for distribution to the townsfolk. In about 1902, they began to install a series of pipes from the main line to private homes.

This distribution franchise passed through several hands, finally with a resident whose heirs assumed the responsibility and interests. In January

1955, the AT&SF sold all rights to the dam and the pipeline to a Madrid resident who, in 1969, sold them to a local realtor. Since that time, there had been a continuous hassle over who actually owned the water works and who was responsible for the upkeep, upgrade, purification, replacement of parts, etc. The courts have now ruled that the realtor is the sole owner.

The details behind the various problems regarding the Cerrillos water question have been outlined many times over the past years, as the very life of this community was dependent upon resolution. Finally, in February 1988, the Governor of New Mexico signed a bill granting $450,000 to purchase the entire system from the realtor and make the necessary upgrades to give Cerrillos and the surrounding area the water it needs in order to exist — new pipes, meters and hydrants.

So with its water problem solved, Cerrillos has leaped over another hurdle on its way to the finishing line of survival.

NEWSPAPERS

The Albuquerque Tribune, 7 December 1965: "Off the Beaten Path" (Howard Bryan).

———— 28 October 1968, p. A-1: "Hotel in Cerrillos Burns ..." (Ralph Dohme).

The Cerrillos Beacon, Vol. 1, No. 1. Cerrillos, New Mexico, 20 June 1891.

The Cerrillos Rustler, Vol. 6, No. 51. Cerrillos, New Mexico, 29 June 1894.

The Denver Post, Rambler Section, 22 June 1969, p. 6: "Once-Deserted New Mexico Town Revisited" (Madeleine Ingraham).

East Mountain Telegraph, Vol. 1. No. 4, 23 February 1988: "Cerrillos Awaits Governor's Decision" (Katharine Beebe).

The Indian Trader, May 1986, p. 13: "The Cerrillos Turquoise Mines" (Martin Link).

The New Mexican, Pasatiempo Section, p. 5, 5 December 1965: "Old Palace Hotel reopened ..."

———— 9 June 1968: "Cerrillos's Barren, Dusty Plaza Cleaned Up, Planted With Trees" (Janet Berenda).

———— 27 October 1968: "Cerrillos Mourns Old Friend" (Jim Peeler)

———— 3 June 1970: "Turquoise Trail Fireman Plan 2nd Annual Primavera Fiesta."

———— 15 March 1977: "Early Morning Blaze Destroys Tiffany's Saloon" (Kirk Ladendorf).

———— 27 July 1986: "The Fading Glitter." (Peter Eichstaedt).

New Mexico Business Opportunities News, November 1987.

The Rustler, Vol. 1, No. 3: 19 October 1978.

———— Vol. 1, No. 6: 9 February 1979.

———— Vol. 1, No. 8: 8 April 1979.

———— Vol. 1, No. 9: 8 May 1979.

———— Vol. 1, No. 10: 11 June 1979.

———— 8 July 1979.

———— 8 August 1979.

———— 21 April 1980.

———— 29 May 1980.

Santa Fe Journal North, 17 February 1987: "Major dreams envisioned in Rancho Viejo."

Santa Fe New Mexican, 1 November 1987: "Galisteo Basin Contains Gold Mine of Ruins." (Peter Eichstaedt)

———— 12 March 1988: "Santa Fe jewelers prepare purchase of turquoise mine." (Melissa Adams)

Santa Fe New Mexican Daily, 28 February 1881, p. 4, c.l. (news item)

———— 11 April 1882, p. 4, c. 1-2: "Millionaire Miners."

———— 23 April 1882, p. 4, c. 2-3: "Los Cerrillos."

———— 8 July 1887, p. 4, c. 2: "Score Another Scoop."

———— 24 June 1890, p. 4, c 2: "Cerrillos Scorched."

———— 22 July 1890, p. 4, c 2: "Building Up Rapidly. Modern Business Houses Going Up at Cerrillos."

———— 14 January 1897, p. 4, c. 4: "Smelter at Cerrillos."

———— 27 September 1897, p. 4, c. 3: "Cerrillos Cuttings."

———— 24 December 1900, p. 4, c. 3: "Light for Cerrillos."

———— 4 February 1901, p. 1, c. 5: "The Edison Plant A Success."

———— 11 February 1904, p. 1, c. 4: "Will Be Disincorporated."

———— 10 April 1907, p. 7, c 4: "Cerrillos is a Lively Camp."

Santa Fe New Mexican Review, 6 June 1884, p. 4, c. 2-3: "Our Own Cerrillos."

Santa Fe Reporter, Vol. 3, No. 42, 7 April 1977: "Old Opera House in New Groove" (John Neary).

———— Vol. 5, No. 52, June 1979: "Centennial" (Bertram Gabriel).

MAGAZINES

Andrews, Myrtle. "Fluries of Fortune." New Mexico Magazine. December 1937, p. 16-17, 40-41.

Barrett, William E. "Poet in a Ghost Town." The Catholic Digest. October 1960, p. 93-100.

Boucher, Leonard H. "Ghost Towns I Have Known." Real West, v. 16, No. 172. December 1973, p. 42-43.

Cowan, John L. "The Turquoise Mines of New Mexico." The Great Southwest Magazine. May 1970, P. 41-42.

Huber, Robert. "Fray Angelico Chavez." New Mexico Magazine. March/April 1979, p. 18-23.

Mays, Buddy. "Ghost Town for Sale." Desert, v. 36, No. 5. May 1973, p. 12, 13 and 41

Northnagel, E.W. "Back Road to Yesterday." New Mexico Magazine. April 1958, p. 18-19, 58-59.

Powers, Marcella. "Cerrillos-It Could Have Happened Here." New Mexico Magazine. August 1968, p. 26-28, 36.

"Madrid New Mexico and the Los Cerrillos Mines." Camp and Plant, Vol. II, No. 13, September 27, 1902, p. 297-303. (Lawrence Lewis, Editor)

BOOKS

Bullock, Alice. *Mountain Villages.* Santa Fe: Sunstone Press, 1981, p. 1-6.

Erdoes, Richard. *Saloons of the Old West.* New York: Alfred A. Knopf, 1979, p. 7.

Florin, Lambert. *Ghost Towns of the West.* Seattle: Superior Publishing Company, 1971, p. 608.

Frost, Max and Paul A.F. Walter. *Land of Sunshine.* Santa Fe: New Mexican Printing Company, 1906.

Hayward, J. Lyman. *Los Cerrillos Mines and Their Mineral Resources.* South Framingham, Mass: J.C. Clark Printing Co., 1880.

Jones, Fayette Alexander. *New Mexico Mines and Minerals.* Santa Fe: New Mexico Printing Co., 1904.

Pogue, Joseph Ezekial. *The Turquoise: A Study of Its History, Mineralogy . . .and Technology.* Glorieta, New Mexico: Rio Grande Press, 1972 (reprint of 1915 edition).

Ritch, William G. *Illustrated N.M. History & Industry,* Fifth Edition. Santa Fe, N.M.: Bureau of Immigration, 1885, p. 166-168.

Schroeder, Albert H. "The Cerrillos Mining Area." *Archaeology and History of Santa Fe County,* ed. Raymond V. Ingersoll. Albuquerque: New Mexico Geological Society Special Publication No. 8, 1979, p. 13-16.

Sherman, James E. and Barbara H. *Ghost Towns and Mining Camps of New Mexico.* Oklahoma: University of Oklahoma Press, 1975, p. 38-41.

Silverberg, Robert. *Ghost Towns of the American West.* New York: Thomas Y. Crowell Company, 1968, p. 241-243.

Stanley, F. *The Cerrillos New Mexico Story.* Pep, Texas: April 1964.

Trigg, Maggie Day. *Cerrillos Adventure at the Bar T H Ranch.* Forword by Nancy Green McCleary. Santa Fe: Sunstone Press, 1985.

Weis, Norman D. *Helldorados, Ghosts and Camps of the old Southwest.* Caldwell, Idaho: Caxton Printers, 1977, p. 235-240.

Williams, Jerry L. "Movies Made in New Mexico." *New Mexico in Maps.* Albuquerque: University of New Mexico Press, 1986.

INTERVIEWS

Clark, Don. Turquoise Mine, Cerrillos, New Mexico. 1986 and 1987.

Eckols, Fran. Tiffany Saloon (former owner), Cerrillos, New Mexico. 1986 and 1987.

Mitchell, E.J. What-Not Shop, Cerrillos, New Mexico. 1987.

Montoya, Emma Simoni. "Emma's Building," Cerrillos, New Mexico. 1986 and 1987.

Mora, Mary Tappero. The Cerrillos Bar, Cerrillos, New Mexico. 1986 and 1987.

Sahd, Joe. Cerrillos Cafe, Cerrillos, New Mexico. 1988.

Simoni, Corrina. The Simoni Store, Cerrillos, New Mexico. 1986 and 1987.

Simoni, Edith. The Simoni Store, Cerrillos, New Mexico. 1986 and 1987.

Smith, Patra. The Old Boarding House, Cerrillos, New Mexico. 1987 and 1988.

Weeks, Julia Vergolio. Former Cerrillos Resident, Albuquerque, New Mexico. 1988.

MISCELLANEOUS

Borgrink, Henry, Data Management Coordinator, New Mexico State Department of Education. Letter 11 November 1987.

Cochran, Genevieve Derham. "The Green Children and their Families," from Notes to Nancy Green McCleary, 17 July 1947 (unpublished).

Grove, Pearce S., Becky J. Barnett, and Sandra J. Hansen. New Mexico *Newspapers: A Comprehensive Guide to Bibliographical Entries and Locations.* Albuquerque: University of New Mexico Press, 1975, p. 435.

Heath, Jim. *A Study of the Influence of the Atchison, Topeka and Santa Fe Railroad on the Economy of New Mexico.* A thesis. University of New Mexico. 1955, p. 33, p. 37.

Minutes, Board of Trustees, Town of Cerrillos, from June 1893 to March 19, 1904.

New Mexico State Records Center and Archives, Santa Fe, New Mexico. Miscellaneous records reviewed, 1986 through 1988.

New Mexico State Office of Cultural Affairs, Historic Preservation Division, Santa Fe, New Mexico.

New Mexico State Historical Library, Santa Fe, New Mexico. Miscellaneous records reviewed 1986 through 1988.

Ochoa, Marina, Curator/Archivist, Historic-Artistic Patrimony and Archives of the Archdiocese of Santa Fe. Letter 5 October 1987.

Roller, Twila J., Archivist, Archives, New Mexico Annual Conference. The United Methodist Church, Letter 6 January 1988.

Santa Fe County Administrative Office, Santa Fe, New Mexico. Miscellaneous records reviewed 1987 and 1988.

Smith, Patra: "History of 'La Casa de Paradise'." (unpublished)

Uptegrove, C.W.: Letters to Governor Prince, May 10, 1889, and November 8, 1890.

U.S Federal Census, 1880, 1900 and 1910. Santa Fe County, New Mexico, Los Cerrillos District.

U.S. Federal Census, 1880. Jack County, Texas.

PHOTO CREDITS

PHOTO CREDITS

Photograph	Page #	Photo Credit
Railroad Station Building	46	Courtesy Mary Tappero Mora
School, with classes	47	Courtesy Emma Simoni Montoya
School skeleton	47	Author
Fiesta crowd	49	Author
Fiesta water hose fight	49	Author
TTVFD Building	50	Author
TTVFD, Food Bar	50	Author
Health Clinic, old	51	Courtesy Emma Simoni Montoya
Health Clinic, new	51	Author
Tiffany adobe walls	52	Author
Plaza; gazebo	53	Author
Cerrillos Cafe	54	Author
Opera House	55	Courtesy David G. Kaufman
Palace Hotel grounds	56	Author
Cerrillos Bar	57	Courtesy David G. Kaufman
"Emma's Building"/Simoni Store	58	Author
What-Not Shop	59	Courtesy David G. Kaufman
Old Boarding House	60	Author
Adobe Antiques	61	Courtesy David G. Kaufman
Casa Grande	62	Author
Rancho San Marcos	62	Author
Post Office	63	Author
Sculptor's building	64	Author
Tower House	65	Author
"Hasta la Vista"	72	Author